Sew Fast - Sew Easy

SEW TOYS

RONA KEMP

WARD LOCK

First published in the UK 1995
by Ward Lock
Wellington House
125 Strand
London
WC2R 0BB

A Cassell Imprint

Designed and produced by
Tucker Slingsby Ltd
3G London House
66-68 Upper Richmond Road
London SW15 2RP

A British Library Cataloguing in Publication Data block for this book may be obtained from
the British Library

ISBN 0 7063 7380 4

Printed and bound in Singapore

CONTENTS

Making the Template

All the toys in this book are made from the same simple pattern. The two pattern pieces are shown here at full size. Simply photocopy these pages and cut around the outline to create your own paper pattern.

If you do not have access to a photocopier, make your own copy using tracing paper. Put the tracing paper over the pages and secure the edges with paper clips. Trace around the outlines, using a ruler for the straight lines. Copy all the marks and notes on the patterns, then cut out the pieces.

If you want to make a strong, lasting template which you can use again and again, cut the pattern out in thin card.

See pages 14–15 for instructions on using these templates to cut out the pattern pieces from fabric. Remember that these pattern pieces do not include seam allowances.

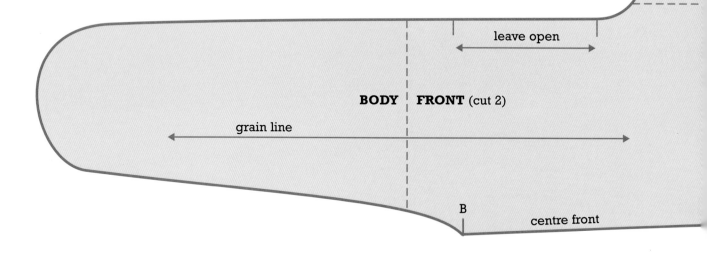

leave open

BODY FRONT (cut 2)

grain line

B

centre front

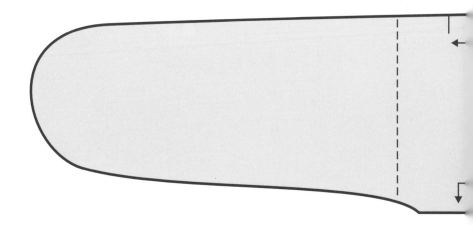

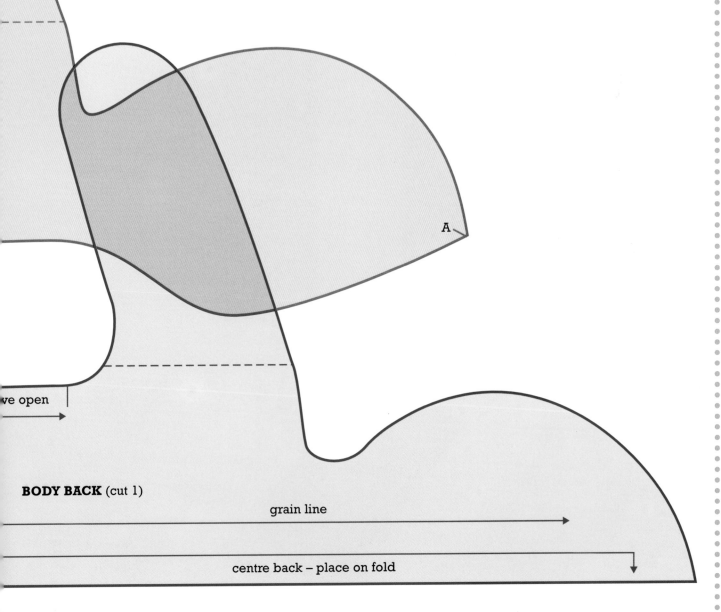

SAFETY TIPS

There are a few simple safety rules to follow when creating your own toys. Make sure that the fabric, fillings and fittings you buy come from an established manufacturer, who will have met legal requirements regarding flammability. Never use toxic paints, inks or dyes. If the toy is intended as a gift for a baby or a small child, do not use buttons, beads or decorations that can be pulled off and swallowed. Remember to check shop-bought eye fastenings to make sure that all the safety plates are securely in place.

A

ve open

BODY BACK (cut 1)

grain line

centre back – place on fold

The Basic Body

Before You Begin

Dolls of every description, from angels and clowns to teddy bears and tigers, can all be made using this one basic pattern. When you have made the fabric body, all you have to do is give your boy or girl doll an appropriate style of hair, face and clothing. To create a cuddly toy, simply add the correct style of ears, tail and face details, following the instructions given.

Basic Sewing Equipment

The equipment you will need to make all these toys is very basic and is probably already in your workbasket:

* Needles in mixed sizes:
  sharps for general sewing;
  crewel needles for
  embroidery;
  long darning needles for
  stitching through the depth
  of the head in working the
  doll's features and hair.
* Stainless steel
  dressmaker's pins.
* Thimble, especially for
  bulky seams.
* Tacking thread.
* Sewing threads in a variety
  of colours.
* Ruler and pencil.
* Air-vanishing pencil or
  tailor's chalk.
* Bodkin or ribbon threader.
* Tape measure.
* Dressmaker's shears for
  cutting out fabric.
* Scissors:
  general purpose scissors for
  cutting paper, cords etc;
  small embroidery scissors for
  neatening threads and
  cutting into seams.
* Tracing paper.

In addition to this basic sewing basket equipment, a simple sewing machine is all you need to stitch the toys. You can make the toys by hand but machining is much quicker. A steam iron and ironing board are useful for pressing seams.

FABRIC

One of the nicest things about making toys of this size, is that you only need small pieces of fabric. You can use leftover pieces, sale remnants, or the little squares of fabric sold as quilters' quarters. For exact fabric quantities see page 14 and individual projects.

Most plain-coloured, lightweight cottons are suitable for the bodies of girl and boy dolls, whereas small prints, checks, corduroys, velvets and fur fabrics are ideal for the animals. If you use velvet or fur fabric, make sure the pile is running downwards from head to tail on all the body pieces.

Thin cottons (such as those used for the rabbits on page 52) are very easy to work with and, if you are not an experienced seamstress, choose a fine cotton for your first toy. You will soon graduate to fur and towelling!

HAND SEWING

Tacking is used to hold together two or more fabric layers temporarily during the construction of a project, usually prior to machine stitching. Use tacking stitches of even length, about 6mm (¼in) apart on areas that require more control, such as curves. Use uneven tacking for long, straight edges, hems and trims.

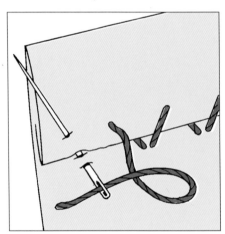

Hemming stitch

This can be used to secure all types of hems and for appliquéing face details. Fold under the turning (no turning on felt), pin and tack in place. Working from right to left, take a tiny stitch in the main fabric and, without pulling the thread through, take another small stitch through the fold of the hem (or felt fabric). Pull the thread through. Insert the needle directly below the first stitch and repeat, spacing the stitches about 6mm (¼in) apart. The stitches above are enlarged for clarity.

Slipstitch

This stitch is used to join two folded edges together. For example, use it to close the gap on the doll's body left for putting in the stuffing. Working from right to left, bring out the thread through one folded edge. Slip the needle through the fold of the opposite edge, for about 6mm (¼in), and bring out the needle. Repeat on the opposite side and continue in this way to the end of the seam.

EMBROIDERY STITCHES

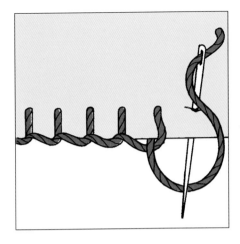

Blanket stitch

Working from left to right, bring the needle out on the bottom line. Insert it above (to the required depth of the stitch) just to the right and bring it out immediately below, with the needle over the working thread. Continue in the same way, making evenly-spaced stitches and keeping the purled edge of the stitch on the outer edge of the fabric.

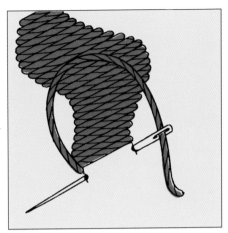

Satin stitch

Working from the bottom left to the top right, embroider straight stitches diagonally across the area to be filled. The stitches should fit close together and be all at the same angle.

Stem stitch

Bring out the needle on the stitch line and make a stitch at a slight angle to the line. Continue in this way noting that the thread always emerges in the middle of the previous stitch.

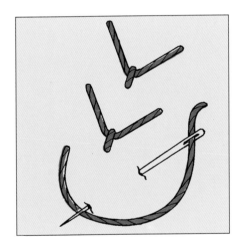

Fly stitch

Bring the needle out at the top left and, holding the thread down with the left thumb, insert the needle to the right, on the same level as the thread. Make a short downwards stitch towards the middle and bring the needle out with the thread below. Insert the needle below the thread. For a mouth, make a second stitch in the centre, then take the needle through to the back of the head and cut the thread close to the fabric.

Chain stitch

Bring out the thread on the stitch line. Holding it down to the left, insert the needle at the starting point and bring it out a short distance below with the thread under the needle. Pull the needle through to form the first link in the chain and repeat as required.

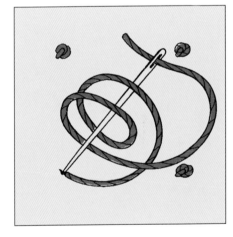

French knots

Bring out the thread where the knot is to be worked. Hold it down with your left thumb and, with the needle, encircle the thread twice. Twist the needle back to the starting point and insert it close to where the thread emerged. Pull the needle through to the back and repeat as needed.

Cutting Out

The basic toy uses just two pattern pieces. The front pattern is cut twice and the two pieces of fabric are sewn together along the centre front to give the face its shape. The pattern for the back of the toy is placed on a fold so the back of the toy is flat, made from a single piece of fabric.

If you are buying fabric to make the body a piece about 80cm x 50cm (32in x 20in) allows plenty over for ears and a tail. See the box (right) for ways to use smaller pieces of fabric.

Using the template to cut out the fabric for your toy's body is easy. For best results, it is important to cut the fabric carefully following a few simple guidelines. Always remember that the pattern you have copied from pages 8–9 does not include any seam allowances.

First of all, press your fabric to remove any creases, especially if you are using fabric remnants, and check that you have sufficient fabric to include seam allowances all round.

Place the two pattern pieces on your chosen fabric in the positions shown below, following the straight grain, which runs vertically down the fabric. This will ensure a smooth finish to the toy. If you cut out the fabric with the pattern at an angle to the grain, the seams may pucker unpleasantly, especially on the face.

If you are using checked fabric, make sure the checks match on the centre front seam. On other patterns, such as paisley prints and flower sprigs, it is worthwhile checking that the front seam looks pleasingly balanced before cutting out the fabric.

USING THE TEMPLATE

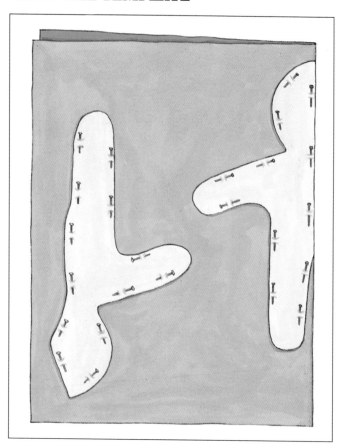

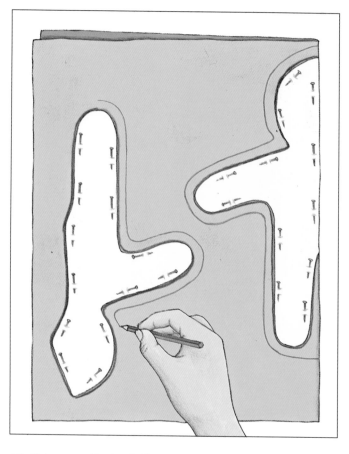

1 With the fabric folded right sides together, pin the back pattern to the fold and the front pattern as shown, on the straight grain of the fabric. Position the two template pieces so that there is sufficient room to add a 1cm (⅜in) seam allowance all round (except on the fold).

2 Using a tailor's chalk pencil or air vanishing pencil, which will not mark the fabric, draw around the pattern. This will give you a clear seam line to follow when you are sewing the pieces together. Draw around the patterns again, adding the 1cm (⅜in) seam allowances as shown.

USING REMNANTS

If you have several small pieces of fabric that you want to use to make a toy, there are various ways you can lay out the pieces. The back of the toy must be cut on a fold, so take the biggest piece of fabric and fold it right side inside. Hold the template against it to check there is enough fabric to allow for the seam allowance.

For the two front pieces, either pin two single pieces of fabric right sides together and cut the fronts that way or, cut them from single layers of fabric, remembering to reverse the template to cut the second piece.

The toys can be made successfully in a wide variety of fabrics.

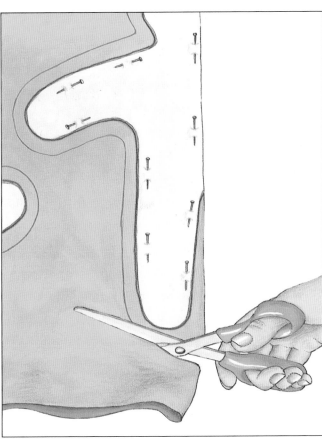

3 Cut out the fabric pieces along the seam allowance line, but do not cut between the legs of the back body piece at this stage.

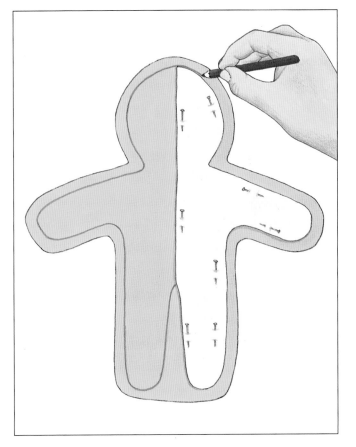

4 Open out the back fabric, reverse the template and repin it on the unmarked side of the fabric. Draw around the template to complete the outline of the back. This will give you a clear line to stitch along.

Sew and Stuff

Before you begin sewing together the fabric pieces for your toy, adjust your sewing machine to make sure you have the right needle, thread and stitch length for the kind of fabric you are using. Test stitch through two layers of the fabric, using scraps left over from cutting out the toy, until you get a good result.

When sewing the body pieces together, it is important to stitch exactly on the seam line (the line you drew around the template) so that the finished toy is well shaped.

Take care to make sure the arms and legs are the same length and width and that the head is evenly rounded. Before you begin stuffing the toy, check that the seam down the middle of the face is smooth and, if necessary, re-stitch to get a

good curve. A toy which is a gift for a young child will get a lot of wear, so it is best to sew round the seam line twice.

For stuffing toys, loose synthetic stuffing is the best choice. This is machine washable and widely available in handy sized bags. Check the stuffing you buy meets legal safety standards, particularly with regard to flammability.

To give a firm, but not too hard, finish to your toy, it is best to tease out the stuffing and use only small amounts at a time. Stuff each piece well into the body with the aid of a knitting needle. Use the blunt end to help push in the stuffing and, at the same time, mould the shape with your hands. Keep checking that the front and back are the correct shape.

Plain and patterned fabrics can make delightful toys. The doll has been made in plain fabric and then painted.

MAKING THE BODY

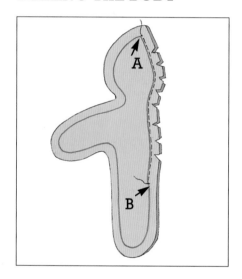

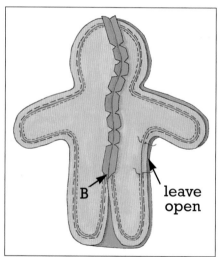

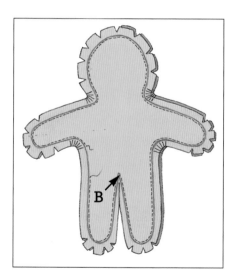

1 With the right sides facing, pin and tack the two front body pieces together. Machine stitch between points A and B, taking a 1cm (⅜in) seam. Remove the tacking stitches. Check the face has a smooth curve. Trim back the seam allowance to 6mm (¼in), notch the curved edge and press open.

2 Pin and tack the front and back body pieces together, right sides inside. Working with the front body facing upwards, stitch around, leaving an opening in one side, as marked, for turning through to the right side. When stitching between the legs, stop and start again at point B: pivot the fabric on the needle, positioning the fabric so that you are ready to stitch the other inside leg seam.

3 Trim, clip into the angles and notch the seam allowances. Cut the fabric between the legs up to point B and trim the seam allowances, tapering them towards the centre. Remove the tacking stitches.

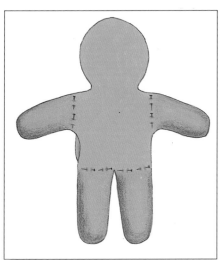

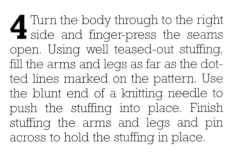

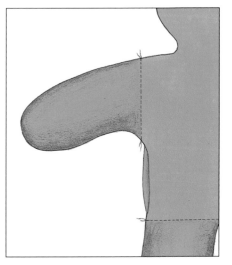

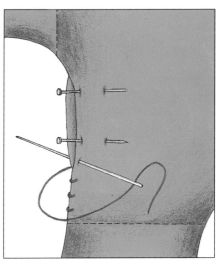

4 Turn the body through to the right side and finger-press the seams open. Using well teased-out stuffing, fill the arms and legs as far as the dotted lines marked on the pattern. Use the blunt end of a knitting needle to push the stuffing into place. Finish stuffing the arms and legs and pin across to hold the stuffing in place.

5 Tack across to form the arm and leg joints. Check the arm seams create shoulders of equal size. Using the zipper foot, stitch across the arms and legs as close as possible to the stuffing. If you haven't got a zipper foot, backstitch neatly across by hand to form the arm and leg joints. Remove the tacking stitches.

6 Stuff the main body, checking that both sides of the body are a good shape. Carefully mould the head, taking extra care to make the stuffing smooth and even in the face. Turn in the seam allowance of the opening, pin to hold the seams together and, using matching sewing thread, slip-stitch to close.

Clothes

Dress

Made from two rectangles of fabric, this little sleeveless dress could not be easier to make. The dress can be lengthened (for example if you want to make a dress that covers the toy's legs completely) and the width increased to make it fuller. The length of the dress can also be extended by adding a deep, gathered frill.

The neck is made by threading elastic through a channel and it is easy to embellish with lace or a separate collar (see page 26).

When choosing a fabric for the dress remember that thin, fine fabrics are easier to use and that small prints look best on small toys. Trims, such as lace, should also be in proportion to the size of the garment so choose narrow lace and ribbon.

You will need
Fabric for dress:
approx 44cm x 20cm
(18in x 8in)
Elastic: 6mm (¼in) wide
Elastic threader
Lace edging (optional)
Ribbon (optional)
Basic equipment (see page 12)

A simple lace collar adds a pretty touch to the basic dress pattern. Note that the dress fabric is also used for the hair ribbon.

BASIC DRESS

1 Cut out two pieces of fabric on the straight grain each approximately 22cm wide x 20cm long (9in x 8in). The exact measurement will depend on the length of dress you want. Seam and hem allowances are included.

2 With right sides inside, pin the two pieces of fabric together. Using matching sewing thread, machine stitch the two side seams 12cm (5in) up from the bottom edge, taking a 1cm (⅜in) seam allowance. Press the seams open.

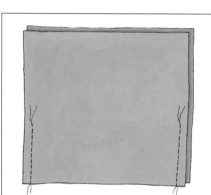

3 The openings above the two side seams form the arm holes. On these edges make narrow double turnings, pin and stitch, tapering the stitching as shown.

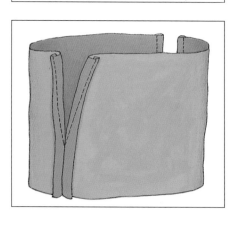

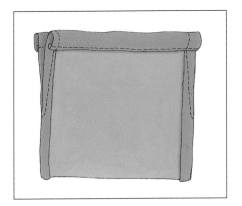

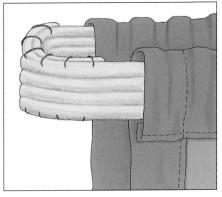

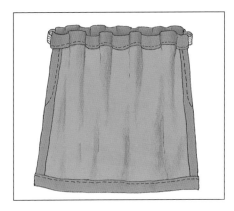

4 On the top edges, make double turnings. First make a narrow turning and then a wider 1cm (⅜in) one. Make sure you have made a channel wide enough for the elastic before you pin and machine stitch.

5 Using the elastic threader or a safety pin, insert elastic through the channel. Draw up the fabric to fit the doll's neck, overlap the ends of the elastic by 2cm (¾in) and oversew around the edges.

6 Hem the bottom edge, first folding over 6mm (¼in) and then 1cm (⅜in). Pin, tack, and using matching thread, machine stitch around.

VARIATIONS

Fabric frill

One way to make a long dress is to add a decorative, gathered frill to the bottom edge, in the same fabric as the dress . You can finish it with a central ribbon bow or fabric rose. For the fabric frill, allow one and a half times the width of the dress by about 10cm (4in). Fold the frill in half lengthways, wrong sides together. Sew a double row of running stitch around the top of the frill through both thicknesses. Pull the ends of the threads until the frill is gathered to the width of the dress. Machine stitch the frill to the bottom of the dress fabric at stage 4, putting right sides together. Press. Finish making up the dress and sew a small ribbon bow or rose to the centre front.

Buttons and bows

For a dress with a decorative bow, cut out and make up as for the standard dress. Thread narrow ribbon instead of elastic through the neck hem. You will need about 50cm (20in) of ribbon. Pull up the gathers and tie the ribbon into a bow at the side of the neck. If the toy is not for a small child, you can add buttons to the front of the dress.

Lace frills

Rows of lace frills make a charming variation on the basic dress shape. First extend the length of the basic pattern by 6cm (2½in). Decide on the number of frills you would like around the bottom of the dress. Multiply the width of the dress by the number of frills, plus one for the collar, to give the total length of lace required.

Make the dress up to stage 4. Do not insert the elastic. Tack and then machine stitch a row of lace to the top edge of the dress making sure the channel is still wide enough for the elastic. This lace will then gather up to form a collar when the elastic is inserted and pulled up.

Starting at the hem, tack and machine stitch lace to the bottom of the dress. Apply more rows to the skirt in the same way, overlapping the edges slightly to give a smooth finish. Finish the ends of the lace neatly. You may like to put one row on the underside of the dress so it peeps out from underneath.

Pants

The basic pants are made from a single rectangle of fabric and can be adapted to make dungarees, trousers with braces (for these add straps made of narrow ribbon) and pantaloons to wear under a dress. For short pants, just roll up the legs of the pants to the length that suits your toy.

Whatever your choice of colour and pattern, it is probably best to use fine or medium-weight fabrics for these small garments. Lightweight fabrics produce less-bulky seams, which makes the handling and finishing much easier.

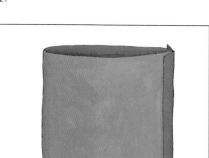

1 Cut out a rectangle of fabric 30cm x 16cm (12in x 6½in) on the straight grain. Fold the fabric widthways in half with the right sides together. Pin and machine stitch the shorter edge taking a 1cm (⅜in) seam. Press the seam open.

2 Make a narrow double hem along the bottom edge, first folding 6mm (¼in) and then 8mm (⁵⁄₁₆in). Pin and machine stitch around.

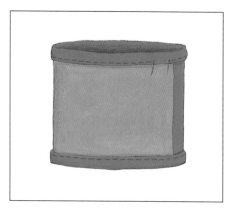

3 On the waist edge, make a similar double turning, first folding 6mm (¼in) and then 1cm (⅜in). Check this is sufficiently wide to insert the elastic, and increase the size of the second turning if necessary.

4 To make the inner leg seam, first measure 6cm (2½in) up from the bottom edge and mark a vertical line down the centre of the fabric.

5 Starting on the bottom hem, about 1cm (⅜in) away from the line, stitch the inner seam. Taper it towards the top of the line. Pivot the fabric on the needle and stitch the second seam, finishing on the hem 2cm (¾in) away from the first seam. Repeat, if needed, to reinforce the seam.

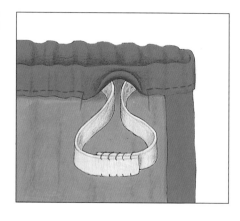

6 Cut along the central line through both layers of fabric. Using an elastic threader or safety pin, thread elastic through the waist edge hem and oversew the ends together. Don't make the elastic too tight or it will squash the toy's body. Turn the pants to the right side and press.

VARIATIONS

Pantaloons

For pantaloons, machine rows of lace on the right side of the fabric before making up. Stitch the first row of lace at the bottom of the fabric rectangle, adding others above so the top edge of the lace is covered each time. For six rows you will need about 2m (2yd) of lace. Then make up the pantaloons in exactly the same way as the pants.

Dungarees

1 For dungarees, cut out the basic pants and a second rectangle of fabric for the bib, measuring 10cm (4in) square. Plus you will need two 14cm (5½in) lengths of 2cm (¾in) wide ribbon for the straps.

2 Make up the pants but do not insert elastic. Fold the bib fabric in half, right sides together, pin and stitch the two short sides taking 1cm (⅜in) seams.

3 Turn through to the right side and press. Turn under the raw edges and, using matching thread, hem the fourth side. Pin this edge to the inside front of the basic pants and stitch across to secure in place.

4 Make narrow turnings on the ends of the ribbon straps and sew them to each top corner of the bib, on the wrong side, neatly hemming them to secure. Cross over the straps and attach the opposite ends to the back inside waist edge.

Trousers with braces

Cut two ribbon braces each about 20cm (8in) long and attach them to the pants front. Cross them at the back and stitch to the back waist edge. You can sew tiny buttons where the ribbon joins the pants if the toy is not for a young child.

A simple rectangle of fabric can be transformed into pretty, lacy pantaloons, brightly coloured dungarees or smart trousers.

Waistcoat

A waistcoat gives a charming finishing touch to many dolls and animal toys. It can be made from any lightweight fabric, but non-fraying felt is the easiest to use and can be decorated with blanket stitch around the edge.

Fabrics that fray are best made into a lined waistcoat, which gives the opportunity to create a really colourful effect with a bright, contrasting lining. Adding a tiny pocket or decorative ties turns a waistcoat into something really special.

You will need
Felt waistcoat
Felt: 30cm x 13cm (12in x 5in)
Embroidery thread

Hemmed or lined waistcoat
Fabric: 38cm x 15cm (15in x 6in)
Lining fabric (optional):
38cm x 15cm (15in x 6in)

Ribbon for ties (optional)
Basic equipment (see page 12)

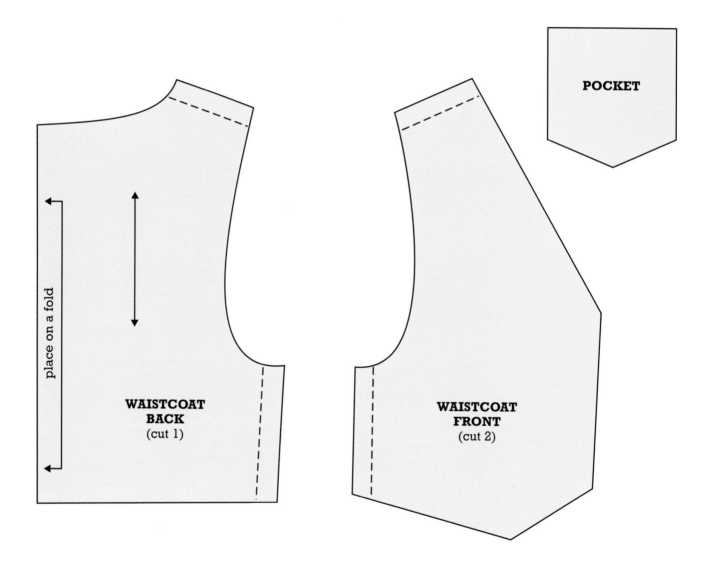

POCKET

place on a fold

WAISTCOAT
BACK
(cut 1)

WAISTCOAT
FRONT
(cut 2)

FELT WAISTCOAT

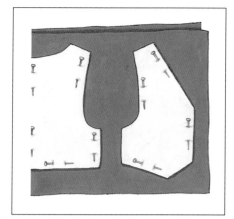

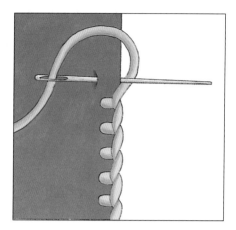

1 For a felt (non-fraying) waistcoat, trace around the waistcoat pattern pieces and cut out a paper pattern. Fold the felt in half widthways and pin the paper pattern pieces as shown. Cut out the pieces carefully to give the felt a straight finished edge.

2 Open out the back section and pin the two fronts in position on the back section, right sides together. Using matching sewing thread, join the shoulders and side seams. You can either machine them or back-stitch by hand. Press the seams open.

3 Using contrast embroidery thread, decorate the edges with blanket stitch (see page 13). Work around the outside edges in one continuous movement, and then stitch around the two armholes to finish the garment.

VARIATIONS

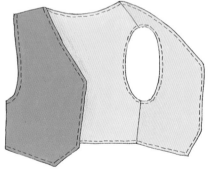

Hemmed waistcoat

To make a waistcoat out of fabric that frays, place the pattern on your fabric as for the felt waistcoat, but add a 1cm (⅜in) seam allowance all round when you cut it out (except for the centre back, which is placed on the fold). Join the sides and shoulders as for the felt waistcoat. Notch the curved edges, turn under all the raw edges and tack. Working from the right side, top-stitch all round by machine or by hand. Remove tacking.

Lined waistcoat

For a waistcoat with a lining, cut out your main fabric adding a seam allowance of 1cm (⅜in) around the pattern (except for centre back) when you cut it out. Cut out the same pieces from lining fabric. Make up both fabrics as separate hemmed waist-coats (see left), but stop before the topstitching stage. After turning under the raw edges, place the two waistcoats wrong sides together, then pin and tack around. Topstitch through both layers. Remove tacking.

Pocket and ties

For a tied waistcoat front, attach two pieces of narrow ribbon to the centre fronts. Fold under a small turning and hem them by hand to the wrong side. To add a pocket, cut out a piece of felt using the pattern on page 24. Pin the pocket to the waistcoat in the position shown and hand or machine stitch around, leaving the top open. You can tuck in a tiny piece of contrast-ing fabric for a handkerchief if the toy is not for a small child.

Collar

A collar is quick to make and can look very attractive as the only accessory on a toy made from colourful fabric. Or you can make a lace-edged collar to give a touch of luxury to a simple cotton dress. A ruff makes an attractive collar for a friendly fabric animal or for the clown doll on page 37.

For best results, choose lightweight cotton or cotton polyester mixes. White collars are simple and pretty, but plain colours and patterned fabrics work equally well, especially as a contrast lining. For a quick result cut a one-piece collar from felt, which won't fray. Or, fray the edge of a cotton collar to give a raggedy effect.

Sew the finished collar to the toy. Remember that small, loose bits of clothing or buttons used for decoration are not suitable for toys made for young children.

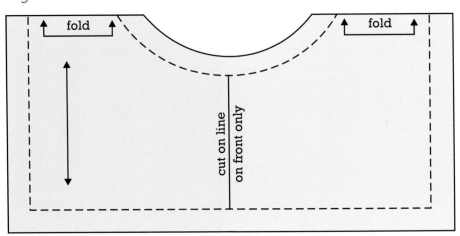

COLLAR

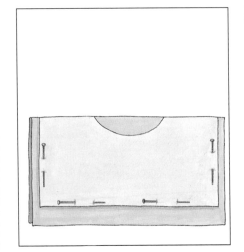

1 For the basic collar, trace around the template and cut out a paper pattern. Fold the main fabric in half. Pin the paper pattern on top, matching the folds, and cut out. Repeat for the lining fabric.

2 On both fabrics, open out the collar and cut along the centre front only. Clip into the neck seam allowance, and fold a 6mm (¼in) turning to the wrong side on all edges.

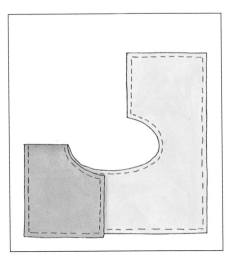

3 Pin and tack both pieces together with the wrong sides inside. Working from the right side, topstitch around all edges either by hand or machine. You can use matching or contrasting thread.

Buttons and bows

You can decorate a plain collar with tiny buttons if the toy is not for a young child. Vary the effect by using contrasting buttons or sewing with contrasting thread. To add ribbon ties to a plain collar, sew about 15cm (6in) of very narrow ribbon to each side of the collar front at the top. These can then be tied together in a bow.

Lace-edged

For a lace-edged collar, allow sufficient narrow lace to cover the outside edges and around the neck, plus a little extra for neatening the cut ends. Make up the collar using the basic instructions, but before topstitching, pin and tack the lace in place between the two pieces of the collar, turning under the raw edges. Working from the right side, topstitch around in a continuous movement.

RUFF

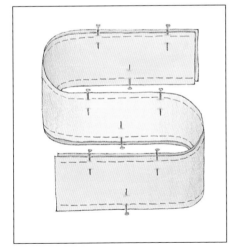

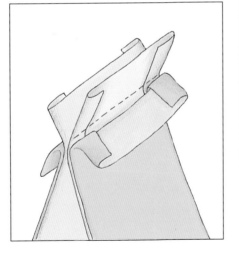

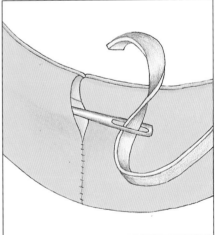

1 For a gathered ruff with a contrast lining, cut two long strips each measuring 56cm x 6cm (22in x 2½in). With the rights sides together, pin and stitch the two long sides, taking 6mm (¼in) seams, to within 6mm of each end.

2 Turn the tube through to the right side and press flat. Fold width-ways in half, right sides together, and stitch the inside seam. Press the seam open and tuck the ends into the gap between the layers. Turn under the remaining seam allowance.

3 Pin to hold and slipstitch the seam, leaving a small opening. Thread elastic through the opening, overlap the cut ends and oversew to secure. Finish slipstitching the seam. Topstitch the lower edge of the ruff to give a neat finish.

Apron

You can make either a simple half apron, or one with a bib and ribbon ties. It can be short or long, lace-edged or plain. You could also give your doll's apron a roomy pocket and, if the doll is not intended for a very young child, you can tuck in a folded checked hankie, a tiny bunch of fabric flowers or a small bunch of herbs for the country look.

1 Cut out a rectangle of fabric for the apron skirt 18cm x 13cm (7in x 5in). You will need a length of matching ribbon – about 70cm (28in) – for the ties.

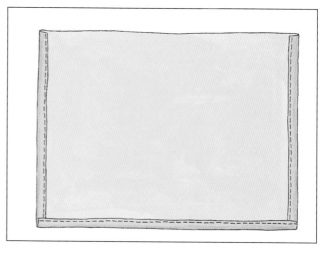

2 Neaten the two short sides of the fabric with a narrow double turning, stitching either by hand and using small running stitches, or by machine. Turn up the bottom edge in the same way.

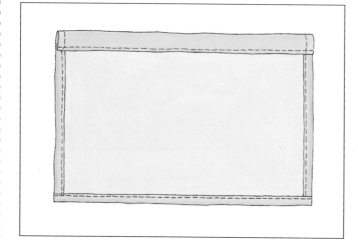

3 Finish the waist edge with a double turning wide enough for the ribbon to be threaded through.

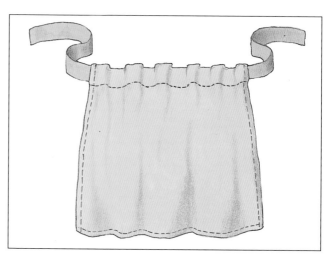

4 Using a safety pin, insert the ribbon through the waist hem. Gather the apron to fit the front of the body and tie around the doll's waist, finishing with a bow at the back. Neaten the ribbon ends.

Long, lace-trimmed apron

For a traditional, 'old-fashioned' look, extend the apron length to that of the toy's dress, which should also be long. Make up in exactly the same way as the basic apron. Add a lace edging to the bottom hem, first tacking the hem and then tacking the lace on from the right side. Machine stitch the lace and hem in place at the same time. Remove tacking stitches and press.

Matching bib

A matching bib with ribbon straps can be attached to the waist edge of the apron following the instructions for the bib of the dungarees on page 23. Attach the ribbon straps, which should be about 25cm (10in) long, in the same way, and tie them in a bow behind the toy's neck.

Pocket

You can also add a decorative pocket to the apron. Cut a square of matching fabric 5cm x 5cm (2in x 2in). Turn a double seam under the top of the pocket then turn under the remaining three edges, tack and press. Pin to the apron skirt and stitch in place, either by machine or by hand.

Dolls

Hair

There is a huge range of possibilities when it comes to making hair for your dolls. Take into account whether the toy is for a young child or a mascot for an adult or teenager. A doll for a very young child may be better off bald – then there is no risk of pieces of hair coming off and being swallowed. A little girl may well prefer traditional long hair made from knitting yarn. For an older child or adult, you can let your imagination roam free!

Rug wool, knitting yarn (plain, textured and lurex mixes), rag strips, embroidery threads, fur fabric, purchased synthetic hair from craft stores – there is an amazing variety of material available.

New yarn will produce straight hair which can be plaited, tied in bunches, or swept up and tied on top of the head. Unravelled knitting yarn makes wonderful curly hair. Mohair gives a delightfully fuzzy finish. You can also embroider loop stitch all over the toy's head to produce a mop of tight curls, while tiny, torn strips of fabric knotted into or sewn on to the fabric of the head create a delightfully old-fashioned doll.

UPSWEPT STYLE

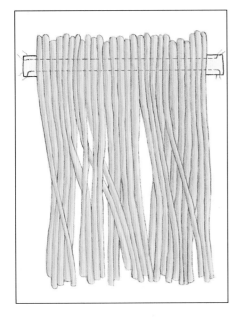
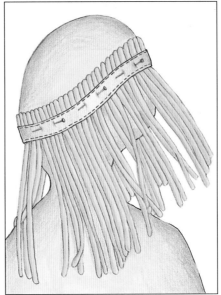
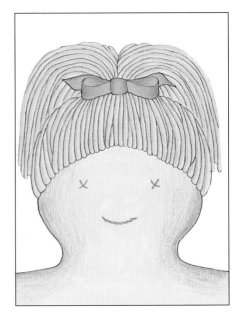

1 For an upswept style, you will need 36cm (14in) of 1cm (⅜in) wide tape, and the yarn of your choice cut into sufficient 23cm (9in) lengths to cover the length of tape. Place the lengths of yarn very closely together along the tape as shown and tack to secure. Working with the yarn uppermost, machine stitch along both edges of the tape.

2 Pin the tape around the doll's head following a line around the forehead and the back of the neck, with the yarn hanging downwards. Overlap the ends of the tape and pin. Hold the doll upside down to check the hair is evenly positioned around the face then, using matching thread, backstitch the tape to the head.

3 Gather the hair on top of the head and tie very firmly around with a piece of the same yarn. Wind the yarn round several times before knotting it securely. Then you can add a pretty ribbon or cloth bow to match the doll's dress.

PLAITS AND BUNCHES

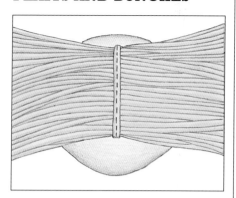

1 Cut 45cm (18in) lengths of yarn. Lay the strands parallel to each other. When you have enough to cover the head from the forehead to the centre back of the head, tie the strands loosely with a doubled piece of the same yarn. Backstitch or glue the hair along the top of the head.

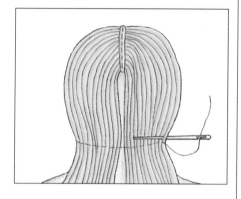

2 Spread the yarn out so that it covers the back of the doll's head. Backstitch it in place to create a hair-line on the back of the head.

3 Divide the hair equally and plait each side, holding the ends with a bow made of ribbon. For bunches, divide the yarn equally and tie each bunch with ribbon.

SHORT HAIR

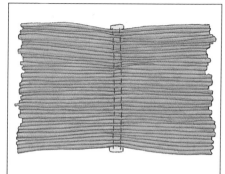

1 For a short hairstyle you will need yarn cut into 18cm (7in) lengths and 13cm (5in) of 1cm (⅜in) wide tape. Lay the strands of yarn parallel to each other across the tape and, working yarn side up, machine stitch along each edge of the tape.

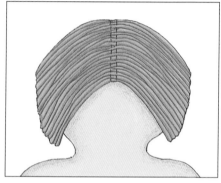

2 Using fabric adhesive, or stitching by hand, attach the tape to the head, from the centre back of the head to the top of the forehead.

3 Trim the yarn to unequal lengths and unravel some of the yarn to give crinkly curls. Cut the front strands to form a fringe if preferred. Using spots of adhesive, stick strands of yarn around the face and neckline to finish.

VARIATIONS

Knotted hair

Tear lightweight fabric into strips about 1cm (⅜in) wide and cut them into 10cm (4in) lengths. Using a large-eyed needle or elastic threader, thread the strips through the head taking a small stitch. Unthread the needle and secure the fabric with a reef knot. Cover the hair area, spacing the knots about 1cm (⅜in) apart. If it is difficult to pull the 'hair' through the body fabric, you can knot it and sew each knot in place on the head.

Embroidered loops

Using several strands of embroidery thread or wool in the needle, work loop stitch evenly over the hair area. Make two back stitches in the same place. Do not pull the first stitch through but leave a loop and secure it with the second stitch, pulling the thread tight before continuing with the next stitch.

Curls

For rows of tight curls, wind yarn around a ruler and secure each loop with back stitching. Slide the loops off the ruler and secure them in rows across the head with back stitching or fabric adhesive. Repeat until the head is covered. Finish with smaller curls around the face, made by winding yarn around a pencil.

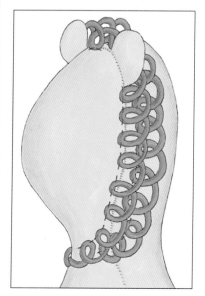

Faces

Face details are the most important way of establishing your doll's character. Always try out eyes and mouths in different positions before making the final decision to sew or glue them in place. The eyes usually look best halfway down the face and about 5cm (2in) apart, but put them on after you have positioned the hair as this will affect the finished look. Place the mouth about halfway below the centre. The nostrils, if any, are best as tiny dots midway between the eyes and the mouth. Cheeks should be added to the sides of the mouth, a little below and wider apart than the eyes.

The main ways of making features are with felt, with simple embroidery stitches or with fabric pens or paint (see page 40). Remember, you can mix and match and have felt eyes with embroidered cheeks and a fabric-painted mouth. This is a good way to create interesting facial expressions.

For safety reasons, buttons should never be used as eyes on toys that may be played with by babies or children under four. Safety eyes are available in a wide range of colours from craft stores. Follow the manufacturer's instructions carefully and see page 44 for further details.

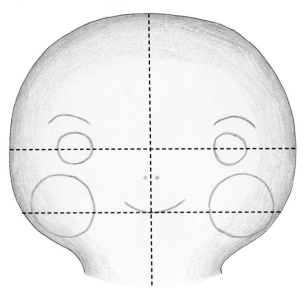

FELT FEATURES

You will need
Scraps of felt
Felt pen
Fabric adhesive
Basic equipment (see page 12)

Felt is ideal for making eyes, cheeks and mouths. It is important to keep the shapes simple. Draw around coins to make appropriately sized circles. Use circles about 1.5cm (⅝in) in diameter for eyes and 2cm (¾in) in diameter for the cheeks. A simple triangle is best

for the mouth because smaller bits of felt may fray. Pin the features in position and check the effect before gluing or sewing in place. Gluing, then hemming around the edges of the felt will ensure that the features stay in place for a long time.

Pieces of felt, buttons, fabric paint and embroidery stitches can be used to create a range of fascinating faces.

EMBROIDERED FEATURES

You will need
Embroidery thread in
appropriate colours
Basic equipment (see page 12)

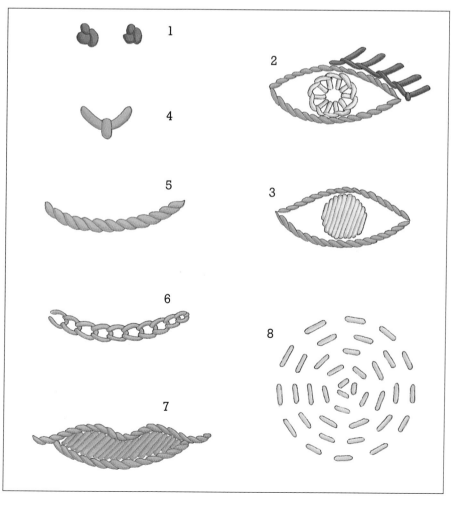

Using an air-vanishing pencil or pins, mark in the features. With one or two strands of embroidery thread, carefully work the features, choosing an appropriate embroidery stitch.

Simple eyes can be indicated with french knots (1) or two single cross stitches. Create a more sophisticated look by outlining eyes in stem stitch and filling in the pupils with blanket stitch (2) or satin stitch (3). Eyelashes can also be suggested with blanket stitch and eyebrows sketched in with a line of stem stitch.

Mouths can be indicated with a single fly stitch (4) or a curved line of stem (5) or chain stitch (6). For a fuller mouth, outline the shape in stem stitch and fill in with satin stitch (7).

French knots can also be used for nostrils. Cheeks can be suggested by cross stitches or by outlining the circle and filling in with a spiral or circles of running stitches (8).

Rag Dolls

This enchanting trio of rag dolls illustrates the great versatility of the basic doll pattern. And remember, you can mix and match fabrics and features yourself to create your own unique dolls. For example, make a rag doll dressed to match a little girl's own favourite outfit or create a boy doll in the colours of the local football team; use old fabrics, or new fabrics deliberately 'distressed', to create and dress an 'antique' doll. The possibilities are endless.

The central girl doll is wearing a short dress to show off her lacy pantaloons. Her dress has a lace collar to match. The boy doll on the left is wearing trousers and a waistcoat and has a little cloth tie made from a scrap of fabric. The clown on the right has upswept hair, cut short and made from multi-coloured wool. He is wearing dungarees with big felt 'buttons' and a spotty ribbon bow tie.

GIRL DOLL

You will need
Fabric for body
(see page 14)
Fabric and lace for dress
(see page 20)
Fabric and lace for
pantaloons
(see page 22–3)
Loose synthetic stuffing
Yarn and tape for hair
(see page 32)
Embroidery thread for eyes
Felt for cheeks
Fabric adhesive
Hair ribbon
Basic equipment (see page 12)

1 Make up the body following the instructions on page 16. Make yarn hair following the instructions for upswept hair on page 32. Look for yarn with a colour variation woven into it as this makes for more realistic and attractive hair.

2 This rag doll has cross-stitch eyes and felt cheeks. Use black or dark blue embroidery thread to make the eyes. Mark the position of the eyes with pins or an air-vanishing pencil, then thread a long darning needle and knot the end of the thread. Insert the needle into the head under the hairline near the forehead. Bring it out ready to make a cross stitch in the correct position. When you have made both crosses, take the thread through to the back of the hair and finish off firmly. The cheeks can be stuck in position or sewn in place.

3 Following the instructions for the dress (page 20) and pantaloons (page 23), make the clothes and dress the doll. The doll can be undressed and dressed so it is easy to give her a change of clothes!

BOY DOLL

You will need
Fabric for body (see page 14)
Fabric for pants and waistcoat
(see page 22 and 24)
Loose synthetic stuffing
Yarn and tape for hair
(see page 32)
Embroidery thread for eyes
Felt for features
Fabric adhesive
Basic equipment (see page 12)

1 Make up the body following the instructions on page 16. Make yarn hair following the instructions for short hair on page 33. Don't always choose black or brown yarn for hair – yellow or red wool gives a fun effect.

2 Cut out and glue on felt eyes and embroider a mouth and cheeks following the instructions on page 35.

3 Make the clothes as shown on pages 22 and 24. A little knitted or fabric scarf in the team colours makes this doll a perfect team mascot.

CLOWN

You will need
Fabric for body
(see page 14)
Fabric for dungarees
(see page 23)
Loose synthetic stuffing
Yarn and tape for hair
(see page 32)
Felt for features and buttons
Fabric adhesive
Ribbon for bow tie
Sequins or beads (optional)
Basic equipment (see page 12)

1 Make up the body following the instructions on page 16. Make yarn hair following the instructions for upswept hair on page 32, but use shorter lengths of yarn. Try mixing strands of different coloured yarns or use multi-coloured yarn for the clown.

2 Cut out clown features in felt and pin them in place. When you are happy with the effect, glue them in position. You can oversew them too if the toy is likely to be subjected to lots of cuddles!

3 Follow the instructions for dungarees on page 23. You can sew big felt patches on the dungarees for an untidy clown or add a smart bow tie and large felt buttons topped with sequins or beads for a well-dressed clown. Remember, sequins and beads won't be suitable for a young child's toy.

Angel

You may want to put this angel on top of your Christmas tree, but she will also find a home at the foot of any little girl's bed. Put a pocket on her dress and this angel can double as a tooth fairy. As a special touch, pop a little star or heart in her pocket.

Look carefully and you will see that the angel has been made so that her face is created on the flat side of the head rather than on the rounded side. This gives her a different look, in keeping with the simple cloth dolls made in the last century.

You will need
Fabric for body
(see page 14)
Fabric and lace for dress
(see page 20)
Fabric for wings:
52cm x 38cm (21in x 15in)
Wadding for wings:
52cm x 20cm (21in x 8in)
Loose synthetic stuffing
Scraps of fabric for hair
(see page 33)
Buttons or felt for eyes
Felt for cheeks
Fabric adhesive
Basic equipment (see page 12)

1 Make the body (see page 16). For hair, tear strips of fabric and knot them in the centre. Sew each knot in place until the head is covered. Note this hair and the button eyes make the doll unsuitable for young children.

2 Use buttons for the eyes and felt for the cheeks. Pin the features on first to check their position before sewing them in place.

3 Using the pattern on page 20 make a long dress with lace collar. If you want the doll to carry a star or heart, sew a large pocket on the dress using a hemmed square of fabric.

4 Make a paper pattern of the wings from the template given opposite. Fold the wing fabric in half widthways and place the paper pattern on the fold. Cut two wings from fabric and one from fabric wadding. Pin and tack the wadding between the fabric wings, then machine stitch all around.

5 Sew the wings to the back of the doll with a few stitches at the back of the neck and where the wings touch the arms. Once the wings are sewn on, you cannot take off the doll's dress. An alternative is to fix them on with press studs or touch and close tape.

The rich colours of the angel's hair and dress add to its charm.

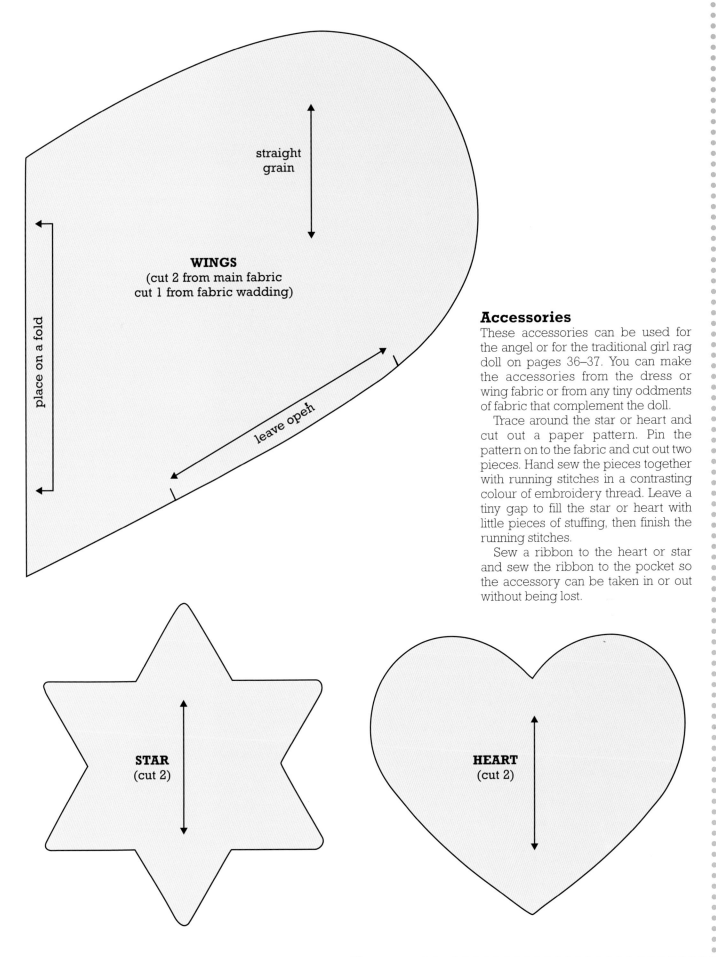

straight
grain

WINGS
(cut 2 from main fabric
cut 1 from fabric wadding)

place on a fold

leave open

STAR
(cut 2)

HEART
(cut 2)

Accessories

These accessories can be used for the angel or for the traditional girl rag doll on pages 36–37. You can make the accessories from the dress or wing fabric or from any tiny oddments of fabric that complement the doll.

Trace around the star or heart and cut out a paper pattern. Pin the pattern on to the fabric and cut out two pieces. Hand sew the pieces together with running stitches in a contrasting colour of embroidery thread. Leave a tiny gap to fill the star or heart with little pieces of stuffing, then finish the running stitches.

Sew a ribbon to the heart or star and sew the ribbon to the pocket so the accessory can be taken in or out without being lost.

Painted Doll

Fabric paints offer great scope for achieving quick, colourful effects that would take much longer using fabrics and thread. A wide range of safe (non-toxic), completely washable and easy-to-use fabric paints is available. Fabric paints can be used for toys and mascots for older children and adults, but should not be used on toys for children still at the sucking and chewing stage! Shoes and stockings, underwear, clothes, facial details and hair can all be created. You can either paint all the clothes and features on to your doll or use fabric paint to create part of the doll's wardrobe – perhaps painted-on underwear and shoes, under a fabric dress.

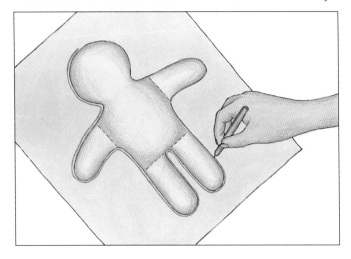

1 Make up a fabric body in a light-coloured fabric following the basic doll instructions on page 16. Then, before painting the actual body, try out several ideas for clothes and faces on paper using coloured crayons or felt pens. Begin by tracing around the body: place it on a piece of paper and, with a light-coloured crayon, trace the outline. Repeat this several times.

2 Experiment with different combinations of clothes. T-shirts and shorts, socks and sneakers, dungarees, sweaters and cardigans can all be painted to suggest plain and patterned clothes for boy and girl dolls. Try out some different ideas for hair styles, facial expressions and features at the same time.

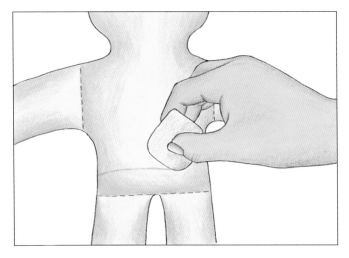

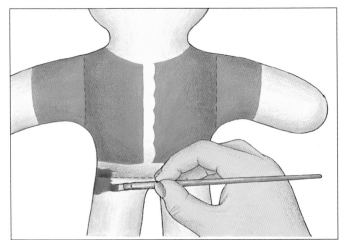

3 Once you have decided on the clothes and features for your doll, transfer the main outlines to the back and front of the fabric body using tailor's chalk or an air-vanishing pencil. Remember to protect your work surface with a sheet of newspaper.

4 Following the manufacturer's instructions, test the fabric paints on scrap fabric so that you become familiar with the technique. Then begin painting in the background colours. Wait for each colour to dry before applying the next otherwise the paints may run into each other.

You will need
Fabric for body
(see page 14)
Loose synthetic stuffing
Drawing paper
Coloured pencils or felt pens
Fabric paints or pens
Paint brushes
Buttons for eyes and shoes
Beads for decoration (optional)
Ribbon for hair (optional)
Basic equipment (see page 12)

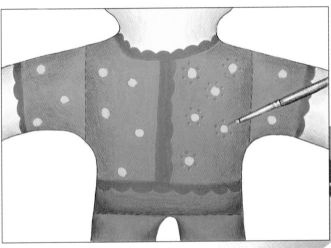

5 When the background colours are dry, add the details. For the doll shown here, use a smaller brush and a dark colour to give the doll's top and pants a lace edging. Paint light-coloured spots on her top and encircle them with tiny spots in the darker colour. Add striped stockings and shoes to complete her garments.

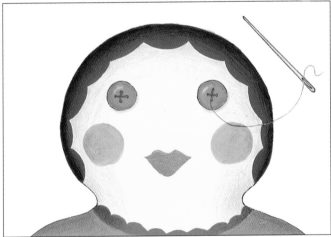

6 Paint the hair and add red cheeks and a mouth. Sew on blue buttons for the eyes. You can also add buttons on the shoes. Decorate her top with beads and stitch a ribbon bow to the side of her head to finish.

Teddy Bears
and
Cuddly Toys

Heads and Tails

Here are a variety of ways of making and attaching eyes, noses, mouths, ears and tails. If you are making a toy for a young child be sure to choose suitable and safe eyes, sew on any features such as ears or feet very, very securely and never use pipe cleaners or wire inside a tail. It is best to choose a very simple tailless toy, such as the duck or a traditional bear, for a young child.

The safest way of creating features for cuddly toys is with simple embroidery stitches. For mascots and toys for older children, fabric pens are a quick and effective way of making faces for some animals, but they are only really effective on pale fabric. Felt features are successful for most toys and are quick and easy to make. They can be glued or sewn in position and it is easy to try them out in different positions before finally fixing them in place.

Marking the features

Before you apply the face details, mark their positions on the toy using an air-vanishing pencil or pins pushed into the toy so the pin heads mark the spot. As a general guide, place the eyes just above the halfway line and 4cm–6cm (1½in–2½in) apart. Keep in mind that eyes placed too close together will give an unfriendly look to a cuddly toy or teddy bear. Position the nose just below the bottom of the eyes and the mouth just below that.

EYES

For felt, button and embroidered eyes, see page 34. Buttons are great for beady animal eyes but safety must always be taken into account. Safety eyes are traditional for teddy bears and will look good on a mouse, cat or dog too. Made from coloured plastic, they are available in a wide range of colours and sizes.

Safety eyes

Always follow the manufacturer's instructions very carefully when inserting safety eyes, which are fixed in place before the toy is stuffed. Push the prong of the safety eye through the fabric in the position desired and secure firmly with the locking device supplied by the manufacturer.

Combined safety noses and whiskers for a variety of animal faces are also available and are

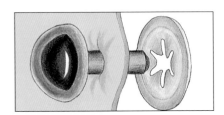

inserted and secured in the same way as the eyes. Manufacturer's instructions should always be read carefully and followed whatever form of feature you are using.

NOSES AND WHISKERS

For embroidered noses and whiskers, mark the position you want and, with embroidery thread in the appropriate colour, work the nose first in satin stitch (see below). Then embroider the whiskers in stem stitch and finish by working two small stitches over the last stem stitch. See page 13 for details on embroidery stitches. Take the needle out through the face and cut the thread close to the fabric.

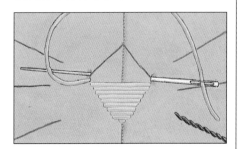

Felt noses are very easy to apply either with glue or hand sewing. Make a paper template if necessary and cut it out. Pin the template on to the felt and carefully cut out the shape using sharp scissors. If you are using fabric adhesive take care not to use too much or it will spread on to the toy. For hand sewing, pin the nose in place and, using matching sewing thread, neatly stitch around the edge of the felt (see below).

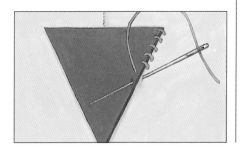

TAILS

Tails, such as the pig's corkscrew tail or the rabbit's pompom, are an essential part of an animal's character. Tails can be made from knotted cord, plaited yarn or a stuffed tube of fabric. Always keep safety in mind for young children's toys.

To make a fabric tail, cut out the tail in the correct fabric using a paper pattern copied from the template, if provided, or simply cut

EARS

Ears can be lined with a contrast colour, as used for the rabbits' ears on page 52, or made from a single layer of felt, as for the tiger on page 50. Ears can be stitched to the outside of the head, where it is easier to adjust the position, or inserted into the seam line as the body is made. For very young children avoid ears which may come loose if the toy is loved too much!

Lined ears

For a lined ear, cut out two ear pieces. These can both be cut from the main body fabric, or you can cut the back from the main fabric and choose a contrasting lining. Sew on to the head or insert in the seam.

1 Make a paper pattern traced from the ear outline given for each toy. Pin it to the chosen fabric and cut out, adding a seam allowance of 1cm (⅜in) as you go. With right sides inside, pin together one piece of main fabric and one piece of lining fabric for each ear. Tack and stitch around the curved edges only.

2 Trim the seam allowances, notch the curved edges, turn through to the right side and press. Turn in the raw edges of the opening and slipstitch to close. Using pins, mark the correct ear positions on the head, spacing them evenly apart. With matching thread and hemming stitches, sew the ears securely to the head or insert in the seam as the toy is made (see below).

Sewn-in ears

If you want to insert the ears into the seam, first make the ears as previously described or cut them from a single layer of felt, remembering to add

a seam allowance to the straight edge only. With the front body pieces right side up, place the ears on the head with seam allowances matching and angling them slightly inwards.

If you have made lined ears, place them with the lining facing the body fabric. Tack across. Then tack the two body sections together and turn through to check the ears are in the correct place before machine stitching the body in the usual way.

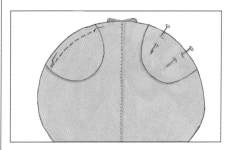

MOUTHS

Mouths are best made by embroidering a gentle upward curve, although some animals such as the lion, teddy bear and rabbits have a central line coming down from the nose. Mark the position and, with the appropriate embroidery wool or cotton, bring the needle out under the nose.

Work the central line first, in either chain or stem stitch. At the bottom, insert the needle and bring it out at the side of the mouth. Complete the mouth and finish as for the whiskers.

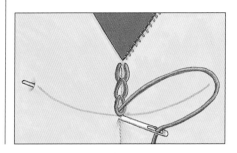

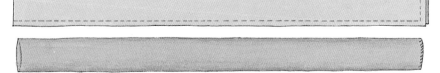

a rectangle of fabric. Remember to add seam allowances. Fold the tail lengthways in half, pin and stitch.

Trim the seam, turn through to the right side and lightly stuff with loose stuffing. Use a knitting

needle to help push it to the end. Turn in the raw edges of the opening and slipstitch to close. Pin the tail to the base of the body and, using hemming stitches, attach it securely in position.

Traditional Teddies

A well-loved teddy is the one toy that many of us keep into adulthood. A handmade bear may not have the lasting qualities of a manufactured one but it certainly scores on individual appeal and charm. Plus you can make a whole wardrobe of clothes for this teddy-boy or teddy-girl to wear.

The two bears photographed here illustrate the very different effects that using different fabrics can create. The bear made in light-brown needlecord with checked paws and inner ears is the ideal bear for an adult or older child. (Lots of adults do like cuddly toys!) The bear made in candy-pink brushed cotton is great for a younger child. But do use safety eyes and check ears are sewn in very securely if the bear is to be a gift for a young child.

Bears can also be made using velvet, velour, fur fabric and – for stylish bears to match your decor – try using leftover curtain or cushion fabric for a flowery, keepsake bear. For information on using fur fabric, see the instructions for the koala.

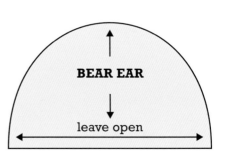

BEAR EAR

leave open

cut 2 from main fabric
cut 2 from lining fabric

BEAR PAW

cut 2 from lining fabric

<table>
<tr><td>

You will need
Fabric for body
(see page 14)
Scraps of fabric for ear
lining and paws
Loose synthetic stuffing
Black felt for nose
Safety eyes or buttons
Black embroidery wool or
cotton for mouth
Fabric adhesive
Basic equipment (see page 12)

</td></tr>
</table>

1 Trace around the ear outline on page 46, adding a 1cm (⅜in) seam allowance all round and cut out. Using this as a pattern, cut two ear pieces from the main body fabric and two from the lining fabric. If you don't want ears lined in contrasting fabric, cut four ears from the body fabric.

2 With right sides inside, pin together one piece of main fabric and one piece of lining fabric for each ear. Tack and stitch around the curved edges only. Trim the seam allowances, notch the curved edges, turn through to the right side and press. Turn in the raw edges and slipstitch to close.

3 Cut out a fabric body using the basic pattern instructions on page 14. Join the two front body pieces. With the front body right side up, position the ears following the instructions on page 45. Then sew together the front and back body pieces.

4 If you are using safety eyes for a young child's toy (see page 44), they should be inserted following the manufacturer's instructions before stuffing the head. Buttons should be sewn on after the head is stuffed. Try them in different positions before stitching very firmly in place. Never use buttons for young children's toys.

5 For the contrasting paws, trace around the pattern, add a 1cm (⅜in) seam allowance and cut out. Pin the paper pattern to the contrast fabric and cut out two paws. Snip into the curved edges, fold under a single turning all around and tack. Pin the paws in place on the inside of each arm and, using matching sewing thread, slipstitch to secure.

6 If your bear wants a nose, cut out a small triangle from dark-coloured felt. Stitch it to the face using matching thread or glue in place.

7 Embroider a curved mouth, if desired, below the nose using black embroidery wool or cotton. Chain stitch (see page 13) works well.

Choose your fabric to match the tastes of the bear's intended owner.

Koala and Keepsake Bear

Here is a real contrast in styles: a cuddly koala made in soft fur and a sophisticated keepsake bear made in floral fabric. The jolly koala will be popular with adults and children alike while the keepsake bear makes a perfect gift for a teenager or adult.

If you have never worked with fur fabric before, do have a go. It is not difficult and the finished effect is well worth the effort. The main thing to remember is to cut the fabric with the pile of each body piece running in a downward direction. Take care to adjust the stitch on your machine to suit the extra thickness of the fabric. Be sure to do some trial stitching on fur fabric scraps until the stitch is right and holds the fabric firmly.

You will need
Grey fur fabric for body
(see page 14)
White fur fabric for ears
Loose synthetic stuffing
Black felt for eyes and nose
Black embroidery wool
or cotton for mouth
Basic equipment (see page 12)

KOALA

1 Make up and stuff the fabric body using the basic pattern instructions (see page 16) and remembering to cut out the fur fabric with the pile running in a downward direction – from the head towards the feet.

2 Trace around the ear template. Add a 1cm (⅜in) seam allowance and cut out. Using this pattern, cut out four ear pieces. To make up the ears, follow the instructions on page 45, using hemming stitch to attach the ears to the outside of the head.

3 Trace around the nose template, make a pattern and cut out the nose from black felt. Glue or stitch in place using hemming stitches. Using black embroidery wool or cotton, stitch the mouth with a wide fly stitch (see page 13).

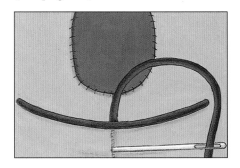

4 To give your koala bear a really furry finish, ease the pile of the fur from the seams using a needle.

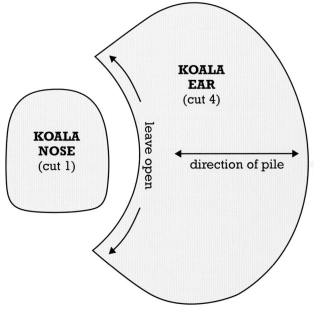

KOALA
NOSE
(cut 1)

KOALA
EAR
(cut 4)

leave open

direction of pile

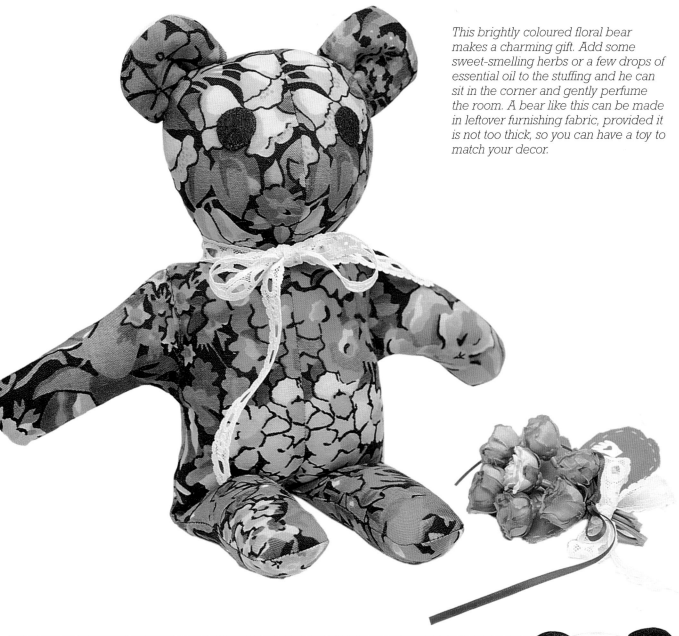

This brightly coloured floral bear makes a charming gift. Add some sweet-smelling herbs or a few drops of essential oil to the stuffing and he can sit in the corner and gently perfume the room. A bear like this can be made in leftover furnishing fabric, provided it is not too thick, so you can have a toy to match your decor.

PANDA MASCOT

The panda has been made from white fabric and then painted with black fabric paint. If you want to make a panda, cut out a white fabric body following the instructions on page 14. Choose fabric that will take the paint well – test it in advance on scrap pieces.

Cut out black fabric ears using the teddy bear ear pattern on page 46 and following the instructions for lined and sewn-in ears on page 45.

Make up the body following the instructions on page 16.

A panda's face can be created either with fabric paints or with black and brown felt and an embroidered mouth.

With non-toxic black fabric paint, carefully paint the arms and legs to complete your panda.

Even though you can purchase non-toxic fabric paints, this toy is not really suitable for children still at the sucking and chewing stage. If you want to make a panda for a young child, cut out felt features and sew them on very securely. Make a black waistcoat and pants (see page 24 and 22) and sew these on to the body. Leave the arms and legs white.

Lion and Tiger

When creating animals, one of the main points to remember is to choose an appropriate colour for the body fabric. The lion, for example, could be made from different shades of yellow, khaki, light brown and so on, and the tiger from fawns and tans as well as the deep orange shown here.

This tiger is made from orange felt which has been fabric painted with black tiger markings. This makes a very striking toy, but not one suitable for a child still at the chewing and sucking stage. In any case, make sure you choose non-toxic fabric paints. For further information on fabric painting, see page 40.

TIGER

> **You will need**
> Fabric for body and ears
> (see page 14)
> Loose synthetic stuffing
> Black felt for nose
> Two black buttons, black felt
> or safety eyes
> Black embroidery thread
> Black and orange yarn for tail
> Black fabric paints
> Paint brushes
> Basic equipment (see page 12)

1 Cut out a fabric body (see page 14). Join the two front pieces (see page 16). Trace and cut out the ear pattern. From a single layer of felt, cut out two ears adding a 1cm (⅜in) seam allowance to the straight edge only. Attach the ears following the instructions for sewn-in ears (see page 45). Finish making up the tiger's body.

2 For the eyes, sew the two buttons in place. If the toy is for a small child you can use two circles, about 1.5cm (⅝in) across, cut from black felt. For the nose, cut a small triangle of black felt. Stick in place with fabric adhesive. Using black embroidery thread, sew in a mouth and eyebrows with stem stitch (see page 13).

3 Following the instructions on the fabric paint, create the tiger's stripes beginning with the head. Paint in the paws and, when they are dry, complete the body, including the back if you wish. Leave the tiger to dry thoroughly. Plait a tail using a mixture of black and orange yarn, following the lion instructions opposite.

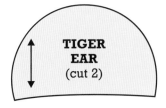

TIGER EAR (cut 2)

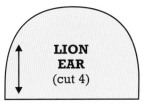

LION EAR (cut 4)

This friendly lion makes a lovable mascot or toy. The unpainted tiger's back (top right), in contrast to his stripy front, shows the very striking effects that can be achieved with fabric paint.

LION

You will need
Fabric for body and ears (see page 14)
Loose synthetic stuffing
Black felt for nose and eyes
Black embroidery thread
Yellow double knitting yarn for mane and tail
Fabric adhesive
Basic equipment (see page 12)

1 Cut out the fabric body in an appropriate fabric, following the instructions on page 14, and join the centre front seam. Trace around the ear pattern, add a 1cm (⅜in) seam allowance all round and cut out. From the remaining body fabric, use this pattern to cut out four ears.

2 With right sides inside, pin two pairs of ears together and stitch around, leaving the straight edge open for turning through. Trim and notch the curved seam, turn through to the right side and lightly press.

3 Attach the ears following the instructions for sewn-in ears (see page 45), then continue to make up and stuff the fabric body following the instructions on page 16–17.

4 Using the double knitting yarn, make the lion's mane following the instructions for curly hair on page 33. Stitch a line of loops around the face, behind the ear and underneath the chin. Continue with several more rows, stitching them close to each other so that the loops stand up.

5 Cut out the eyes and nose from black or brown felt, and stick them in place. Circles about 1.5cm (⅝in) in diameter work well. Embroider the mouth, as for the koala (see page 48).

6 For the tail, cut nine 30cm (12in) lengths of double knitting yarn. Using a large-eyed needle, thread each strand through the base of the body. Pull through until the ends are even and divide the strands into three. Plait to the end and knot to finish.

Rabbits

These rabbits will make a perfect Easter gift. If you are making a rabbit as a keepsake for an adult, add a sprinkling of lavender to the stuffing to make a sweet-smelling present. Choose between an upright or flop-eared bunny. If you find it hard to choose between them, you will just have to make both!

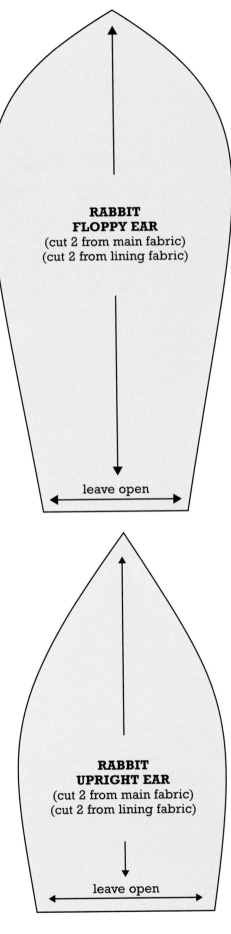

RABBIT FLOPPY EAR
(cut 2 from main fabric)
(cut 2 from lining fabric)

leave open

RABBIT UPRIGHT EAR
(cut 2 from main fabric)
(cut 2 from lining fabric)

leave open

UPRIGHT EARS

You will need
Fabric for body and ears
(see page 14)
Contrast fabric for ear lining
Loose synthetic stuffing
Embroidery thread in appropriate
colours for features
Fabric adhesive
Yarn for the tail
Thin cardboard
Basic equipment (see page 12)

1 Make up the fabric body following the basic pattern instructions on page 16. Trace around the upright ear pattern, add a 1cm (³⁄₈in) seam allowance all round and cut out. Using the pattern, cut two ears from the main fabric and two from the lining fabric.

2 With the right sides inside, pin together one piece of main fabric and one piece of lining fabric for each ear. Tack and stitch around the curved edges only. Trim the seam allowance, notch the edges, turn through to the right side and press. Turn in the raw edges of the opening and slipstitch to close.

3 Pin the ears in position on the top of the head spacing them about 3cm (1¼in) apart. Using matching thread and hemming stitch, sew the ears securely to the head stitching through the seamline. As you sew, slightly curve the outer edge of each ear forward.

4 Cut out two circles from paper, about 1cm (³⁄₈in) across, for the eyes and a triangle for the nose. Position them as shown, pin to hold and draw around with tailor's chalk or mark with pins pushed into the fabric. Using embroidery thread (three strands) fill in the eyes and nose with satin stitch and suggest the mouth with stem stitch. Add the pompom tail.

FLOPPY EARS

You will need
Fabric for body and ears
(see page 14)
Contrast fabric for ear lining
Loose synthetic stuffing
Embroidery thread for features
Fabric adhesive
Yarn for the tail
Thin cardboard
Basic equipment (see page 12)

1 Make up the body as for the rabbit with upright ears. Trace around the floppy ear outline and add a 1cm (³⁄₈in) seam allowance all round. Using the paper pattern, cut two ears from the main fabric and from the lining fabric.

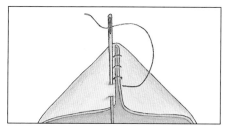

2 Stitch around the ears, turn through to the right side, and close the opening as for the rabbit with upright ears. At the straight end of the ear, fold in the corners to meet in the centre and, using matching thread, slipstitch them to secure.

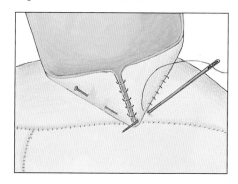

3 Pin the ears in position on top of the head, right sides together and the points towards the front, as shown. Space them about 4cm (1½in) apart and sew them in position with hem stitching. The ears will then fall forward across the face.

4 Stitch the face details and add a little pompom tail, picking out a colour from the main fabric for the tail. Sew on securely.

TAIL

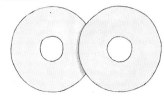

1 For the tail, make a pompom as follows. From thin cardboard cut two circles, 5cm (2in) across and then cut out a 1.5cm (⅝in) wide hole in the middle of each one.

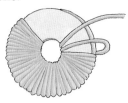

2 Wind the yarn around the cardboard, taking it through the middle and over the edge, until the hole is filled.

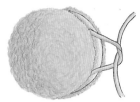

3 Cut the threads around the outer edge. Pull the two cards slightly apart and knot a length of yarn around the threads.

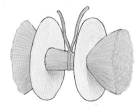

4 Tear away the cardboard circles and trim any long ends.

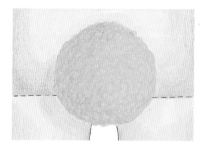

5 Sew or glue the tail firmly to the base of the body.

Cat and Mouse

Traditionally paired together, often as friendly enemies, the cat and mouse make a wonderful addition to your collection of toy animals. They can be made from pretty prints or from more realistic cat and mouse colours. If you choose plain fabrics for the bodies, you can brighten them up with contrasting ear linings and a wardrobe of appropriate clothes.

The cat shown has a wired tail, but for a young child's toy it is easy to leave out the wire and just fill the tail with a tiny bit of stuffing.

A long piece of appropriately coloured cord or ribbon sewn on very firmly, or a plaited tail as for the lion and tiger (see page 50), will suit the mouse and can also be used for the cat if you prefer this to a fabric tail.

CAT

> **You will need**
> Fabric for body and ears
> (see page 14)
> Lining fabric for ears
> Loose synthetic stuffing
> Felt for eyes and nose:
> green, white and pink scraps
> Safety nose and whiskers or
> plastic whiskers (optional)
> Padded wire for tail (optional)
> Ribbon for neck
> Fabric adhesive
> Basic equipment (see page 12)

1 Make up the fabric body following the basic pattern instructions on page 16. Note that a combined safety nose and whiskers should be inserted before stuffing the head. Follow the manufacturer's instructions.

2 Trace around the ear, add a 1cm (⅜in) seam allowance all round and cut out. Using the paper pattern, cut two ears from the main fabric and two from the lining fabric. Make the ears and stitch them to the head (see page 45).

3 For the tail, cut a piece of fabric 25cm x 15cm (10in x 6in). Fold it lengthways in half, right sides facing. Pin and stitch the long side and one short side. Turn through and insert the padded wire to make it curl, or fill it with stuffing. Turn in the opening edges and stitch. Sew to the body.

4 Cut out the eyes and nose in felt and stick or sew them in place. If you haven't used a safety nose and whiskers, back stitch the individual whiskers at each side of the nose or buy and insert plastic whiskers. These are available from craft stores.

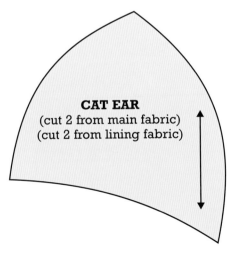

CAT EAR
(cut 2 from main fabric)
(cut 2 from lining fabric)

MOUSE

You will need
Fabric for body and ears
(see page 14)
Lining fabric for ears
Loose synthetic stuffing
Felt for eyes:
green and white scraps
Pink and black yarn for
nose and whiskers
Twisted cord for the tail
Fabric adhesive
Basic equipment (see page 12)

MOUSE EAR

(cut 2 from main fabric)
(cut 2 from lining fabric)

1 Make up the fabric body using the basic pattern instructions on page 16. If you are using fabric with a pile, such as velvet, make sure the pile goes in the same direction.

2 Trace around the ears, add 1cm (⅜in) seam allowance all round and cut out. Using the paper pattern cut out two ears from the body fabric and two more from a contrast fabric. Make up the ears as explained on page 45. Position the ears on the top of the head, spacing them 7cm (3in) apart and stitch securely in place.

3 For the tail, knot both ends of the cord and attach one end to the base of the centre back with one or two oversewing stitches.

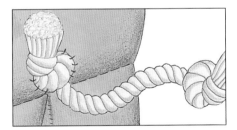

4 For the nose and whiskers, draw in an outline with tailor's chalk and fill in the nose with satin stitch and the whiskers with stem stitch.

5 For the eyes, cut out circles from white and green felt and stick or sew in place.

This dramatic cat (left) has felt features and plastic whiskers. The cuddly mouse has a fabric bow to match his outsize ears.

Dog

This versatile hound looks good dressed in a wide variety of ways and can be given a change of personality with each change of clothes – as the four photographs on the next page illustrate. If you want your dog to wear trousers, you will need to make a small hole in the back of the pants for the tail to stick through. Blanket stitch around this to prevent any fraying.

The dog shown here is made in plain brown fabric with black ears, eyes and tail. But it would look equally good in a spotty fabric.

Take time to get the ears at the right angle. These ears give the dog a lot of personality and need to stick out either side of the head at just the right angle! Plain ears or ears with a lining in a contrast colour will both look good.

You will need
Fabric for body (see page 14)
Contrasting fabric for ears
Black felt for eyes and nose
Loose synthetic stuffing
Fabric adhesive
Tracing paper
Basic equipment (see page 12)

---

1 Make up the body in the fabric of your choice, following the basic pattern instructions on page 16. If you want your dog to have safety eyes (see page 44) you will need to insert them before the body is stuffed. Safety eyes look good on a dog and there are a wide range of colours to choose from.

2 Trace around the ear outline. Add 1cm (⅜in) seam allowances all round and cut out. Using the paper pattern, cut out four ear pieces from your chosen fabric. If you want your dog to have contrast ear linings, cut two ears from one fabric and two from a contrast fabric.

3 Make up the ears following the instructions on page 45 and stitch them securely to the top of the head, spacing them about 5cm (2in) apart. Gather the fabric slightly as you sew. This will make the ears stick out in an appealing way.

4 For the dog's eyes, cut out two circles from black felt each about 2cm (¾in) across. For the nose cut a black felt triangle. Sew or stick these features in place. If safety is not a consideration, dark button eyes suit some hounds.

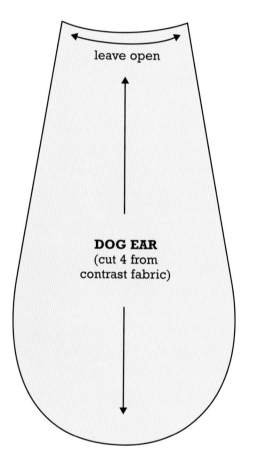

leave open

DOG EAR
(cut 4 from contrast fabric)

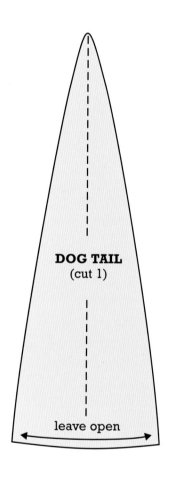

DOG TAIL
(cut 1)

leave open

5 The tail can be made either to match the body fabric or in fabric to match the ears. Trace around the outline given, adding a 1cm (⅜in) seam allowance all round. Using the pattern, cut out the tail and fold lengthways with right sides together. Pin and stitch the long side, leaving the end open.

6 Turn through to the right side and lightly stuff. Turn in the raw edges at the base of the tail and stitch to close. Attach to the back of the body, sewing securely in place.

A sheepskin waistcoat and a ribbon bow tie turn your dog into a real hound about town.

A dog with colourful dungarees is the perfect playmate for a child.

Mistress Dog looks very fetching in a dress with her ears tied up in a matching bow.

A matching waistcoat and trousers make a smart outfit for a dog.

Duck and Pig

These farmyard friends, made in appropriately coloured and textured fabrics, make great gifts. The finishing touches include a curly tail for the pig (not suitable for a toy for very young children) and padded, webbed feet for the duck.

These toys also look great dressed up. Make a pair of pants and matching waistcoat to turn piggy into Master Piglet. The duck looks great in a pair of dungarees or with a jaunty ruff or collar.

The duck and pig shown here have felt eyes but you could also use safety eyes (see page 44) or buttons if the toy is not for a small child.

DUCK

You will need
White towelling fabric
(see page 14)
15cm (6in) square of orange felt
Scrap of black felt for eyes
Loose synthetic stuffing
Tracing paper
Basic equipment (see page 12)

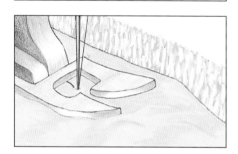

1 Make up the fabric body using the basic pattern instructions on page 16. Should the towelling loops get caught in the machine feed, stitch with tissue paper placed beneath the foot. This is easily pulled away afterwards.

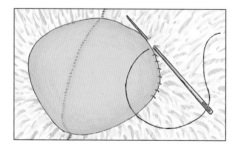

2 Trace around beak outline, adding a 1cm (⅜in) seam allowance and cut out. Using the pattern, cut two pieces from the orange felt. Place together and stitch around, leaving the opening as shown. Turn through to the right side and stuff. Sew in place using hemming stitch. Cut out two small black felt circles for eyes and glue or sew in place.

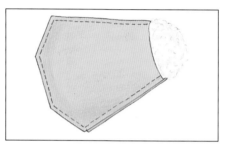

3 Trace the foot outline and, using this as a pattern, cut out four foot pieces from orange felt. Place the pieces together in pairs, pin and stitch around, leaving an opening as shown on the template. Lightly stuff and stitch the opening closed.

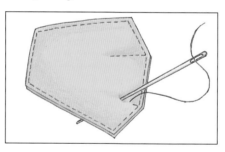

4 Stitch lines to indicate webbed feet. You can do this by hand or by machine.

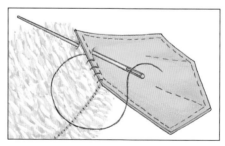

5 Working from the back, pin the feet to the bottom of each leg, with the web foot facing forward and slightly outwards. Stitch to secure.

leave open

DUCK BEAK
(cut 2 from felt)

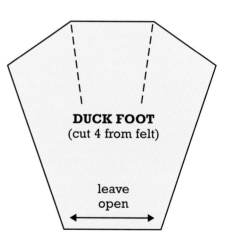

DUCK FOOT
(cut 4 from felt)

leave open

PIG

You will need
Fabric for body, ears and tail
(see page 14)
Pink felt for nose and ears
Black and white felt for eyes
Loose synthetic stuffing
Padded wire or pipe cleaner
for the tail
Black embroidery thread
Fabric adhesive

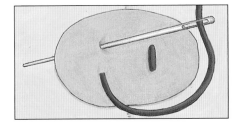

1 Make up the fabric body following the basic pattern instructions (see page 16). Trace around the ear pattern, adding a seam allowance of 1cm (³⁄₈in) all around and cut out. Using the paper pattern, cut out two ears from the body fabric and two from the pink felt. Make up the ears following the instructions for lined ears on page 45. Stitch them securely to the top of the pig's head, spacing them about 4cm (1½in) apart.

2 Trace around the nose outline and, using the cut-out tracing as a template, cut out the nose from pink felt. Pin the nose in place and attach it to the face with two stitches using black embroidery thread. Fasten off neatly underneath the felt.

3 For the tail, cut out a piece of fabric measuring 25cm x 8cm (10in x 3in). Make the tail as for the cat on page 54, putting padded wire or a pipe cleaner inside. To give the tail a corkscrew effect, twist it around a pencil before sewing it firmly in place. If you want to make a pig for a young child it will have to go without a tail.

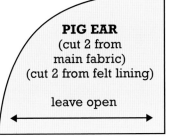

PIG EAR
(cut 2 from
main fabric)
(cut 2 from felt lining)

leave open

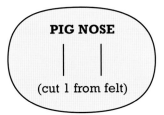

PIG NOSE

(cut 1 from felt)

Lamb

A woolly lamb to love. What child could resist the appeal of this cuddly little toy? Made in synthetic wool-style fabric (available in craft stores and the fabric departments of large department stores), this lamb is delightfully simple and needs nothing more to adorn it than a pair of ears, felt eyes and a ribbon bow. Be warned, because of the thickness of this woolly fabric, the finished toy will be slightly bigger than normal.

You will need
Fabric for body and ears
(see page 14)
Contrasting fabric for ear lining
Black felt for eyes and nose
Loose synthetic stuffing
Fabric adhesive
Tracing paper
Basic equipment (see page 12)

1 Make up the fabric body following the instructions on pages 16.

2 For the ears, trace around the outline, add seam allowances of 1cm (³⁄₈in) all round, and cut out. Using the paper pattern, cut out four ear pieces from your chosen fabrics. Make up following the instructions on page 45 and stitch them securely to the top of the head about 8cm (3in) apart.

3 For the eyes, cut out two circles from black felt about 2cm (³⁄₄in) across. For the nose, cut a small black felt triangle. Sew or stick the eyes and nose securely in place.

4 For the tail, cut a piece of the body fabric 15cm x 8cm (6in x 3in) and fold lengthways, right sides together. Stitch the long side and one short side. Turn in the right way, slipstitch the opening closed and sew securely to body.

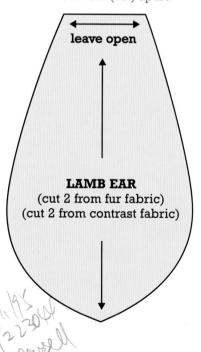

leave open

LAMB EAR
(cut 2 from fur fabric)
(cut 2 from contrast fabric)

Most toys look good in a variety of fabrics but a lamb demands woolly fur fabric.

Index

Acknowledgements

Design Robert Mathias
Photography Jon Bouchier
Step by step illustrations King and King
Templates and patterns Robert Mathias
Editor Dorothea Hall